Imprint

Please visit our website:
www.papierfresserchen.de

Idea and text: Benni Over, Klaus Over
German text revision: Klaus Over, Jennifer Madelmond, Birgit Hock, Steffen Griesinger
Illustrations: Kathrin Britscho, Benni Over
Layout and image design: Jennifer Madelmond
Enquiry: Birgit Saftig, Benni Over, Christine Szyska
ISBN: 978-3-86196-942-6 – Paperback
ISBN: 978-3-86196-971-6 – epub E-Book
ISBN: 978-3-86196-972-3 – PDF E-Book

© 1. Edition 2020 – Papierfresserchens MTM-Verlag GbR
Mühlstraße 20, 88085 Langenargen, Germany
www.papierfresserchen.de – info@papierfresserchen.de

All rights reserved.
Original edition published in 2017:
„Henry rettet den Regenwald".

HENRY SAVES THE RAINFOREST

Benni Over

This is Benni.

He wants to tell you a story about the orangutans. Orangutans are monkeys that live in the rainforests of Borneo and Sumatra and their habitat is under threat.

The rainforest is home to countless animals. A green world filled with sounds and life. In Benni's story, a little orangutan named Henry has a grand plan: He wants to save the rainforest.

Henry has this terrible dream over and over. In it, he is still a very small orangutan.

He is happy because his mommy takes good care of him. Right now, she is on her way to find food for them both. All of a sudden Henry is startled by a loud noise. Carefully, he keeps watch. What he sees is as new and scary to him as the loud creaking noise. But the little orangutan can't see his mommy anywhere.

"Mommy, mommy, where are you? Don't leave me alone!", Henry calls out in desperation into the rainforest.

Henry shuffles from branch to branch in panic, looking for his beloved mommy. When he finally finds her, she is lying on the ground. Her eyes are closed.
"Mommy, please open your eyes," Henry begs. But Henry's mommy is asleep. She will sleep forever. Something very bad has happened.

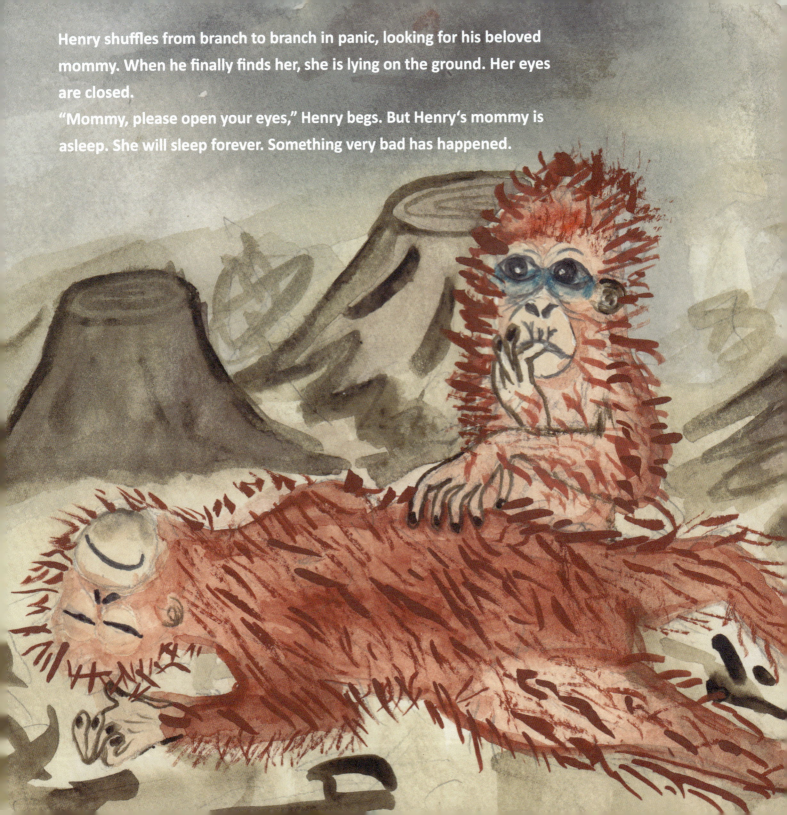

Dripping with sweat and trembling in every limb, Henry awakes out of his dream with a start. He calms down slowly once he realizes that he is in the comforting arms of his human surrogate mother Mary. For more than five years, the animal attendant has been looking after the young monkey, which has grown into an adult male.

"Mary, why don't I have an orangutan mommy?", Henry asks all of a sudden. "Oh, Henry, you were found in a piece of woodlands near a palm oil plantation when you were barely a year old. Your mother was probably killed as she tried to find food on the plantation. Here, in this camp, you have found a new home. You grew up with other monkey children who, just like you, lost their mommy."

"But why are our mommies being killed?", Henry asks in shock.

"This happens because humans are clearing more and more rainforest, destroying the habitat of the orangutans. Some experts claim that rainforest the size of over 200 football fields is being cut down every day," Mary replies. "But why are they doing that?"

"It happens because of money, Henry!" Mary explains. "People are selling the wood and need more and more space for their palm oil plantations."

That's when Henry makes a decision: "This is not right and must be stopped! I will leave and tell the people to stop cutting down the rainforest."

Surprised at so much courage, Mary says: "Perhaps this really is the only way, Henry! Do you know that you have a godfather in Germany? His name is Benni and he loves the rainforest as much as you do. Maybe he can help you with your mission."

The next morning before sunrise, Henry sits next to Wang Yong in an old van, completely focused on his task, as it rattles on bumpy roads through the rainforest. Wang Yong is Mary's friend. He supports Mary and the monkeys whenever he can. But in this case, he finds Henry's mission too risky and hopeless. He says to Henry skeptically: "How is that supposed to work? Come on, Henry, how are you going to manage the long journey to Germany – and just think, what can an individual like you accomplish?"

But Henry can't be talked out of it: "I can do this! And Benni will help me to find people who support me. It is not right that the rainforest is being cut down and that orangutans are losing their habitat. I will tell that to everyone!"

Shortly afterwards, Henry is sitting in a propeller-driven plane that takes him to Singapore. Although the pilot can't believe his eyes at first, he lets the hairy woodsman on board and advises him to take a cruise ship in Singapore for the onward journey to Germany.

When Henry sees the big white ship in the port of Singapore, he becomes discouraged a little. But he can't give up now! Very quickly, he climbs up one of the thick ropes of the ocean liner and hides beneath the tarpaulin of a lifeboat. His journey continues from Singapore to the port of Hamburg.

Henry is travelling for a whole 53 days.
Fortunately, he has packed enough bananas.

Finally, having arrived in Germany, Henry observes from his hiding place that all the people get off the ship. But how is he supposed to get off the ship now? He looks along the edge of his lifeboat and sees a narrow branch without leaves beneath him.

The little orangutan gathers all his courage and dares to take the leap into the unknown … Phew, that was a near miss. He slides down the smooth, strange-looking branch and suddenly finds himself standing in the middle of a small sailboat.

"Hey, who are you?", a surprised voice suddenly asks from behind Henry.
The little orangutan turns around in surprise. "I am Henry and I have to save the rainforest."
"And my name is Florian and I just came back from a fishing trip in Denmark."
Henry tells Florian his story and about his godfather Benni, whom he wants to find.

„No, I don't believe it! You want to go to Benni?", Florian wants to know.
"Yes, why?", Henry asks in surprise.
"You won't believe it, but Benni is my brother! If you want, I will take you to him!"

When they finally reach Benni's house after more than 500 kilometers, the joy is enormous. Benni and Henry hug each other for a long time and then Henry tells about his journey.

The next morning, the two exchange views for hours. They talk about their lives, the situation of the rainforest and the threatened habitat of the orangutans.

Benni is very happy that Henry has come to him and assures him: "I will help you and support your mission!"
"But how are we going to do that, Benni?"
"First of all, Henry, you will have to travel to a lot of people and tell them your story. A movement must be set in motion. You need many allies now!"

"That sounds good, Benni, but where should I start?"
"It is best if you travel to Berlin first, to BOS Germany. The BOS is an orangutan aid organization that collects money for orangutan orphans and buys large areas of rainforest. In these forests the monkeys can live in peace and freedom. Maybe the BOS can also help you making contact with politicians in the German Bundestag," explains Benni. Henry likes the idea and appoints Benni as his personal advisor and ambassador for the orangutans in Germany.

Before Henry travels to Berlin, the newly appointed advisor equips him with important things he can use during his trip: a smartphone, a map and, of course, money.
Furthermore, Henry is accompanied by Benni's favorite cuddly toy, Cinta.

Immediately, Henry calls Wang Yong and tells him about his experiences so far as well as his plan.
But Wang Yong remains skeptical and is concerned.
"Don't overdo it, Henry! I am afraid that this might be too big for you!"
But Henry returns: "Don't worry, Wang Yong. I will arrange something!"

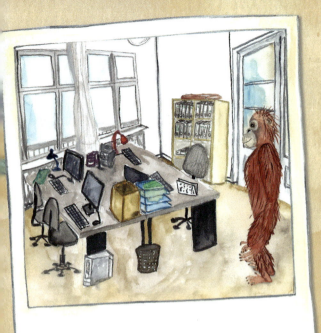

The next day, Henry takes the train to the capital of Germany. Once in Berlin, he meets with employees of BOS Germany. They give him lots of information and help him to arrange an appointment at the German Bundestag so that he can present his case there. Henry is the first monkey who has been permitted to speak in front of the politicians.

A few days later the time has finally come. Henry receives for his mission not only applause from the members of parliament, but also further aid commitments:
The Chancellor personally arranges for Henry to have an audience with the Pope in Rome.

In the Vatican the Pope is already waiting for the little orangutan, happy about this special visit. The Pope can understand Henry's concern.
He describes the clearing of the rainforest as an intervention in God's creation and promises to help the orangutan.

For now, the last stage of his journey takes Henry to America. There he meets the President of the United States at the so-called White House. But even though the President is very friendly and promises to help him as well, Henry begins to doubt his mission, because so far only promises have been made but no one has actually acted on them yet.

So, Henry finally returns to Benni's small idyllic town, sad and depressed. Once having arrived there, he calls Wang Yong at the orangutan camp 15,000 kilometers away and tells him about his doubts.

However, everyone in the camp thinks it is great what Henry is doing.

But Henry remains uncertain.

The following night the little orangutan has a pleasant dream. He dreams of his friends in the camp and of an orangutan mommy who tends for her baby lovingly.

When Henry wakes up from this dream, he feels a new sense of courage. For it has shown him once again what goals he is fighting for. And so he makes a decision: "I want for all orangutans in this world to be able to grow up in peace with their parents. I have to talk to Benni right now and find a solution to finally take action against the deforestation of the rainforest."

Arriving in the garden, Henry bursts out: "It is not enough for everyone to say that they want to do something, but in the end nobody really does anything. People have to start acting together now!"

"Yes, you are right, Henry. It only works when everyone comes together and decides something together", Benni confirms. "We have to find a way to organize a world conference with all governments!"

"How is that supposed to work and how can one orangutan bring the governments of the world together?" Henry asks, taken aback.

"You already have so many allies," Benni says. "But you need one more advocate that many people in the world listen to: the Dalai Lama! Because the Dalai Lama is a Nobel Peace Prize winner who is already over 80 years old and who is committed to solving the world's conflicts in a peaceful manner."

A few hours later Henry has already boarded a plane to travel to India. Benni has told him that the Dalai Lama lives in the village of Dharamsala at the edge of the Himalaya. Once there, he tells him about his mission.

Henry also tells him that he has doubts about his mission.

The Dalai Lama looks at him for a long time. He is impressed by so much courage and touched by Henry's immense compassion for his fellow orangutans.

"Henry, what you are doing is good and important! Because what you do to others, you also do to yourself. The harm that humans are inflicting on orangutans will eventually fall back onto them. If you save the orangutans, you will also save the humans. They have to understand that."

Henry feels the power of his words, but before he can say anything in return, the Dalai Lama gives him one last piece of advice: "Tell your story! That is how you will reach people."

As he leaves, the Dalai Lama winks at the little woodsman and says with a smile: "And, Henry, let's arrange something!"

After more than 100 days, Henry returns to the island of Borneo and goes to the orangutan camp, his home. He is very tired and still has great doubts if he could achieve anything with his journey. The only thing that cheers him up is the fact that he can soon play with his friends again and will finally be able to sleep in his own tree nest.

But when he finally arrives, he feels that something is wrong. The camp is empty and none of his friends are there! "Hello? Where are you? Mary? Wang Yong?" Desperately, Henry searches the whole camp for his friends.

All of a sudden he hears strange noises from afar. The orangutan has a presentiment and hurries in the direction from which the noises come. "Oh no! I am too late!"

He sees the machines, uprooting trees and tearing up the ground only a few hundred meters away from the camp. Henry is petrified with horror. All his efforts had been in vain.

But then he notices something that almost takes his breath away. All the local people and orang-utans in the area have joined together to form a long chain of monkeys and humans, trying to push back a bulldozer. Wang Yong stands in the middle of the chain and leads the group. When he spots Henry, he smiles and calls out to him:

"Hey, Henry! Good to see that you are back! Come here and help us. Thanks to your journey we have come to realize that even an individual can achieve something by joining others." Monkeys and humans stand side by side, holding each other's hands. Together they manage to stop the bulldozer and even push it back.

When the annoyed workers finally abandon their plan and drive away with their machines, the joy is immense. Everybody cheers and they gather around Henry and carry their widely travelled friend on their shoulders and back to camp.

Mary joins them excitedly. She tells them that she has just received a call from Germany. The BOS Foundation was able to buy the land behind the camp.

That evening Henry calls Benni and tells him what has happened, beaming with joy as he does so. Benni is happy that the little orangutan has arrived home safely and that the bulldozers had to stop the deforestation.

A week later Benni receives a package from Henry. He opens it and finds his beloved stuffed animal Cinta inside. Benni discovers the beautiful postcard then, written in Henry's scrawly handwriting:

Benni, when are you coming to visit me? Let's arrange something!

WE WILL ARRANGE SOMETHING!

What can be done

In order to save the rainforest, everyone has to help, because everyone can do something to preserve the rainforest as well as the habitat of the orangutans. For example, pay attention to the products in which you can find palm oil as an ingredient. Of course, this does not mean that you have to stop eating chocolate spread on your bread just because it often contains palm oil. But more and more manufacturers are starting to use only palm oil that does not require the destruction of more rainforest. You can also donate a tree to help Henry and Benni with their mission.

The donated tree will be planted by the BOS* Foundation for reforestation on cleared and protected areas. The orangutans and, of course, Henry will thank you for this!

* The BOS ("Borneo Orangutan Survival") is a nature and species conservation organization that protects orangutans and their habitat. The achieve this not only through educational work, but also by working in two rescue stations on Borneo. There, young orangutans are prepared for their life in the wild.

Benni and Henry

Benni has a big dream: He wants to protect the orangutans and their habitat. Nothing can stop him, neither the wheelchair and his illness nor the long distance to Indonesia, which he travelled to meet Henry (see picture).

For years, Benni has been campaigning for the interests of the orangutans and tries to make other people aware of the existing wrongs. Together with his father Klaus he finally wrote the story of "Henry saves the rainforest", which was first made into a film and now published as a children's book. With his gripping and touching mission Benni has been able to inspire countless people and build up a huge network of allies.

Furthermore, three partnerships between Indonesian and German schools were established. Because, as Wang Yong has learned throughout the course of the story, every single person can do something for a better world, and that is exactly what Benni fights for every day.

Printed in Poland
by Amazon Fulfillment
Poland Sp. z o.o., Wrocław